You Are a Robin!

LAURIE ANN THOMPSON

ILLUSTRATED BY **JAY FLECK**

 DIAL BOOKS FOR YOUNG READERS

You are a robin!

You are inside an egg, but it is time to come out.
You take your first breath and

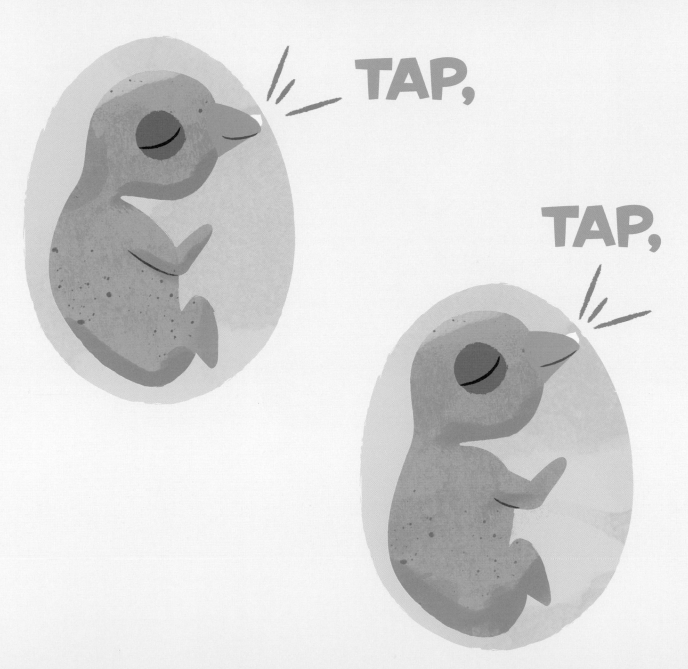

TAP,

TAP,

TAP, with your special egg tooth.

TAP! TAP! TAP!

You
PECK,

TURN,

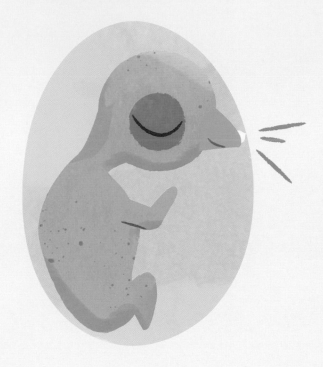

and
PUSH

for hours,

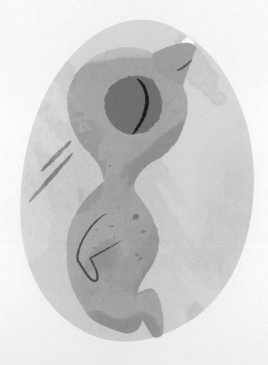

until finally . . .
crack!

PECK!

TURN!

PUSH!

The top of the eggshell lifts off.

You are wet and naked!
You can't see.
But you are not alone.

Your mom takes away your eggshell.
Your dad lands on the edge of the nest.

You **POP** up,

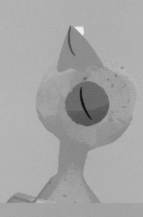

You **OPEN** your mouth wide,
and **WAIT.**

Soft, warm food drops in.

Yum!

POP!

OPEN!

WAIT!

It starts to rain.

You and your new siblings
SHIVER.

Mom sits with you.

You
SNUGGLE
under her wings.

Finally, you are warm again.

You SLEEP.

You are growing fast!

At one week old, your eyes open and you have feathers.

At two weeks, you are almost as big as your parents.

You are ready to leave the nest.

You
FLIT,

FLAP,

FLUTTER
to the ground.

FLIT!

FLAP!

FLUTTER!

Dad drops an earthworm at your feet
instead of into your mouth.

You **GAZE** at it,

GRAB it with your beak,

and **GULP** it down.

Dad is teaching you to hunt.

One day he sounds
the alarm,

"Chuck,
chuck,
chuck!"

A cat!

You
HOP
away.

It comes closer.

You
JUMP
to a branch.

You
FLY
away, just in time.

It jumps too!

Dad dives at it, snapping his beak.

HOP!

JUMP!

FLY!

Summer is here.

You
BATHE
in puddles

and
PREEN
your feathers.

You
SNAP
at spiders

and
CRUNCH
up crickets.

SNAP!

PREEN!

BATHE!

CRUNCH!

It gets colder.
More and more robins join your flock,
but there is less and less to eat.

It's time to leave for winter.

You

FLY . . .

and

FLY . . .

farther than you have
ever flown before.

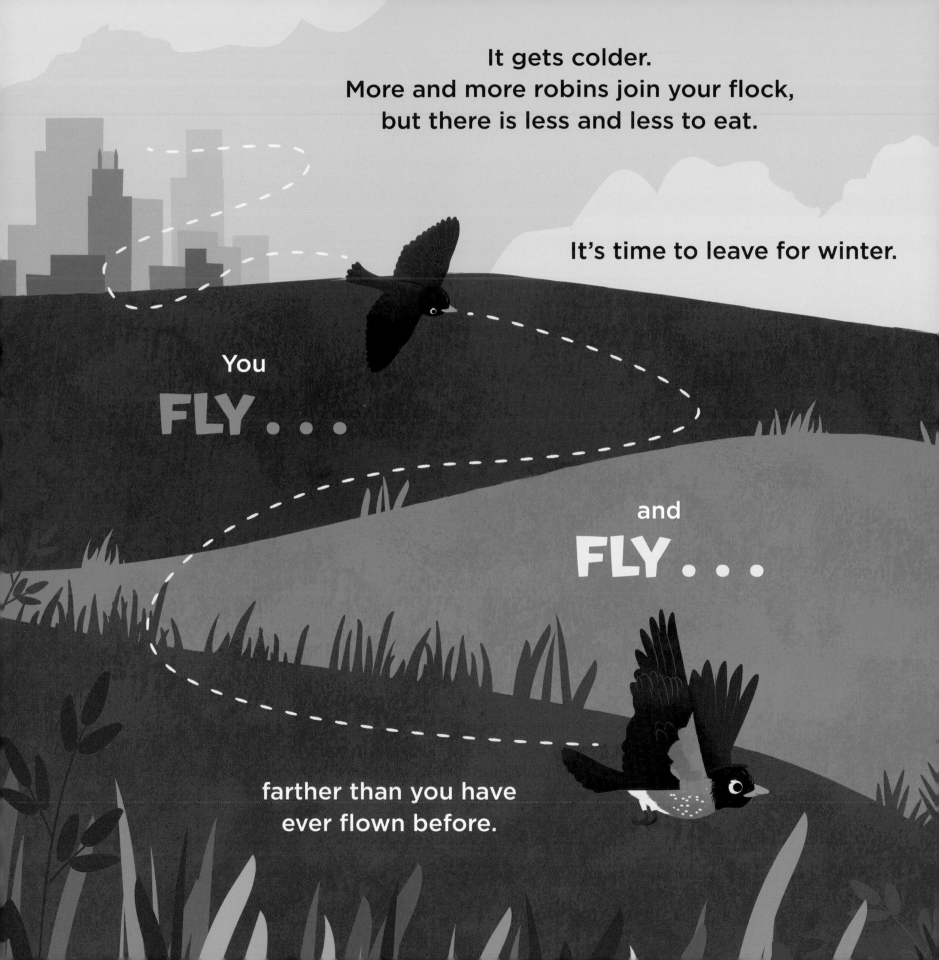

When you arrive,
the food is different.

You
BITE
into berries.

You
CHEW
on cherries.

BITE!

FLY!

FLY!

CHEW!

After a few months, it's time to go home.
You fly and fly.

Finally, you
STOP.

You
LOOK
for a good place to live.

You
LISTEN.

A male robin is singing.
You have found your place.

STOP!

LOOK!

LISTEN!

It's time to build your nest. You choose a sturdy pine tree.

You and your mate

CARRY

twigs, moss, and string.

You

WEAVE

them together
into a bowl.

You
FILL
it with mud,

then
SMOOTH
it with your chest.

FILL!

WEAVE!

CARRY!

SMOOTH!

Your nest is finished.

You **SIT,**

STAND,

and finally

PUSH.

An egg!

SIT!

STAND!

PUSH!

You do this once each day until
you have four blue eggs.

Now you rest.

You

SIT,
SIT,
SIT,

on your eggs.

You warm them when it is cold.
You shade them when it is hot.

You roll them over,
so they stay just right.

SIT!

SIT!

SIT!

You

WAIT, WAIT, WAIT.

WAIT!

WAIT!

WAIT!

After about two weeks you hear a tap, tap, tap.

Your first chick is coming out of its egg.
You will take good care of it, because you are a

Fun Facts About Robins:

The American robin is one of the most common and easily recognized birds in North America, and they are fascinating to learn about!

Robins don't usually go back to the same place year after year. They go wherever they can find food, water, and shelter.

Robins don't always fly south for the winter. As long as they can find food, they may prefer to stay right where they are.

Robins eat more than just earthworms! They also love to eat caterpillars, beetles, flies, spiders, grasshoppers, and more. They eat a wide variety of berries and fruits too. Their diet changes depending on the seasons and what they can find.

If a robin is in danger, it will call out for help. Nearby robins will rush in to assist.

Both parents help raise babies, and each parent does specific jobs. They work hard to help their babies thrive.

Glossary:

EGG TOOTH: A small, hard bump on the tip of a baby bird's beak. It is used to break through the eggshell so the bird can hatch.

FLOCK: A group of birds gathered together

MATE: A partner in raising babies

PREEN: To clean and smooth one's feathers

Be a Robin!

Draw a circle on a piece of paper. Use a pen or pencil to poke holes along the line. How many holes do you have to make before you can push out the circle? This is how a robin gets out of its egg.

Collect twigs, pine needles, string, yarn, and/or grass. Try to weave a bowl with your supplies. Are you a good nest builder?

If a robin can't find mud for inside her nest, she makes some! Find some dry dirt outside. Add water! Mix the dirt and water to make a soft, strong mud for building.

Without moving your head, look up, then down, then side to side. A robin can't move its eyes like you can, so it has to move its whole head to look at something. Try looking at the same things again, but this time move only your head.

A robin can eat up to fourteen feet (more than four meters) of earthworms a day. Have a grown-up help you measure that distance. That's a lot of worms! Can you guess how many?

Robins love to bathe and preen their feathers. Enjoy a nice bath. Don't forget to comb your hair afterward!

Why Robins Are Important:

People love robins! Many of us enjoy watching and listening to them in our backyards and parks. Seeing the first robin of spring often makes people happy after a long winter.

The American robin is the official state bird of Connecticut, Michigan, and Wisconsin.

Robins eat insects and other creatures that people believe to be pests.

Robins eat fruits and berries, which helps spread those seeds to new places.

How to Help Robins:

Many robins are hurt by house cats. Keep your pet indoors if possible, and make sure it wears a collar with a bell.

Robins need fresh water for bathing and drinking. Put out a shallow dish or bird bath for them to visit.

Robins don't usually like birdseed. Instead, put out fruit, berries, or mealworms for them to eat.

Plant berries and fruit trees for robins to eat from, and other trees for them to nest in.

In spring, leave out short pieces of string, ribbons, or yarn for robins to use for nest building.

If you see a nest, try not to go close to it until the birds have moved on.

Ask your parents to limit the use of chemicals used near your home.

Support organizations that help birds, like the National Audubon Society (audubon.org) and the Cornell Lab of Ornithology (birds.cornell.edu).

FOR ELAINA —L.A.T.   **TO AUDREY —J.F.**

With special thanks to Dr. Andrew Farnsworth at the Cornell Lab of Ornithology

Dial Books for Young Readers
An imprint of Penguin Random House LLC, New York

First published in the United States of America by Dial Books for Young Readers, an imprint of Penguin Random House LLC, 2024
Text copyright © 2024 by Laurie Ann Thompson • Illustrations copyright © 2024 by Jay Fleck

Dial & colophon are registered trademarks of Penguin Random House LLC. The Penguin colophon is a registered trademark of Penguin Books Limited.
Visit us online at penguinrandomhouse.com.
Library of Congress Cataloging-in-Publication Data is available.
Manufactured in China • ISBN 9780593529751
1 3 5 7 9 10 8 6 4 2
TOPL

Design by Sylvia Bi • Text set in Gotham • The illustrations were created digitally.